Polar Worlds

With special thanks to Birgit Freybe Bateman for her companionship on my polar worlds adventures.
—Robert Bateman

First published in Canada in 2008 by
Scholastic Canada Ltd.
604 King Street West
Toronto, Ontario
M5V 1E1

10 9 8 7 6 5 4 3 2 1

Library and Archives Canada Cataloguing in Publication

Bateman, Robert, 1930 –
Polar worlds / Robert Bateman with Nancy Kovacs.

      1. Animals—Polar regions—Juvenile literature. 2. Animals—Polar regions—Pictorial works—Juvenile literature. 3. Bateman, Robert, 1930– —Travel—Polar regions—Juvenile literature. 4. Polar regions—Description and travel—Juvenile literature. I. Kovacs, Nancy II. Title.

QL104.B38 2008   j591.75'86   C2008-900375-6

ISBN-10: 0-545-99725-9 / ISBN-13: 978-0-545-99725-6

Printed in Singapore by Tien Wah Press

Produced by
Madison Press Books
1000 Yonge Street, Suite 200
Toronto, Ontario, Canada M4W 2K2
madisonpressbooks.com

This book is printed on paper harvested from forests managed with sustainable and environmentally sound practices.

Polar Worlds

Life at the ends of the earth

Robert Bateman

with Nancy Kovacs

A Scholastic / Madison Press Book

Introduction

I love travelling, and have been lucky enough to travel to many parts of the world that are rich in natural beauty and wildlife. I have to confess, though, that I was not expecting much when I made my first journeys to the Arctic and Antarctica. After all, these places have harsh climates, and are very difficult to survive in. How much could there be to see?

I first visited the Arctic as a university student hired to help a geologist map an iron ore deposit. The moment we stepped off the small plane that had taken us to our destination—a remote part of northern Quebec—I was struck by the beauty of the place and by the incredible variety and abundance of wildlife. The plants and shrubs were much smaller than they are in warmer climates, and I felt like a giant in a miniature world. I was immediately charmed, and spent my free hours observing and sketching the many birds and animals I saw there. Each visit has been the same. I have been to many Arctic regions, in North America and in Europe, and the beauty of the Far North remains as thrilling as the first time I saw it.

I visited Antarctica many years later, and, quite honestly, all I expected to see were great expanses of ocean, ice, and mountains, with the occasional glimpse of a distant penguin. I was curious, it's true, but imagine my amazement when I discovered a place of spectacular beauty, teeming with wildlife.

My polar journeys have been highlights in my travels. Getting there is not easy, but the rewards are great. I hope that these pages will be a voyage of discovery for you, and that they will lead you to learn even more about the beauty of the two polar regions.

An Arctic Wolf surveys the vast expanses of an Arctic winter.

In the
ARCTIC

Polar Bears

The Polar Bear is the symbol of the Arctic. This great white carnivore roams the vast ice in search of food. Its huge body is covered in thick, luxurious fur that conserves heat, and has hollow hairs mixed in. Air trapped in its fur helps keep the bear afloat in water. Hair on the pads of its feet gives it the grip it needs to walk on ice. Polar Bears prefer to eat seals, especially Ringed Seals, and they are skilled, patient hunters.

The Polar Bear is probably the most ingenious of Arctic survivors. When it stalks a Ringed Seal, it sometimes pretends to be a chunk of ice drifting slowly in the water toward the ice floe where the seal is resting. Unnoticed by the seal, the Polar Bear stays quiet until it is close enough to grab the seal. Another tactic it uses is to build a wall of snow and hide behind it until a seal comes close.

My family and I once were able to get very close to a Polar Bear enjoying a recently caught seal on an ice floe. As our ship approached, the bear watched carefully, clearly not wanting to abandon its kill. When we got too near, it jumped into the water, swimming alongside the ship for a short time. Finally, it climbed onto another floe, shook the seal in the air, then dove back into the water with its prey and swam off to find a quieter place to eat.

The Polar Bear lives and hunts on Arctic ice. Shrinking ice caps and the warming of Arctic waters are threatening the survival of these amazing hunters.

FACTS About Polar Bears:

- Polar Bears are the world's largest land predators. Males weigh from 775 to more than 1,500 lb (350 to more than 680 kg). Females weigh much less, from 330 to 550 lb (150 to 250 kg).

- Polar Bears are protected from the cold in part by a layer of fat under the skin that can be up to 4.5″ (11 cm) thick. They can maintain their normal body temperature, even when the air is -34°F (-37°C)!

- A bear can eat 100 lb (45 kg) of seal blubber in one meal.

- A Polar Bear's liver contains enough vitamin A to poison a human, so it's best not to eat the liver!

FACTS

About Grizzly Bears:

- The name Grizzly means "gray," and refers to the grayish tips of the bear's fur—this is also the reason for its nickname "the silvertip bear."

- An adult Grizzly can weigh 400 to 1,500 lb (180 to 680 kg) and stand 8 ft (2.4 m) tall on its hind legs. The male is nearly twice as large as the female.

- The large hump over the Grizzly's shoulders is all muscle, which makes its front legs powerful enough to dig for food.

Grizzly Bears

Grizzly Bears, or Brown Bears, live all around the world, both in the Arctic and in temperate climates. They can be very fierce, going to great lengths to protect their food, and a mother will not hesitate to use her long, sharp, powerful claws to protect her cubs from any threat.

Grizzly Bears in the Arctic hibernate during the long winter months. Hibernation is also called denning, because the bears stay in their dens during this time. Their body temperature lowers, and all of their body systems slow down. They have no need of food or drink, and stay in their dens for as long as five to seven months in the coldest winters. In temperate climates, the hibernation is shorter. In their warmest habitats, they may not fully hibernate at all.

Grizzlies are omnivores, like us. This means that they eat all sorts of food, like fish, small animals, grasses and other plants, and even the roots of plants. The same claws that can tear apart a threatening intruder can also dig insects out of rotting trees or small animals out of the ground. Grizzly Bears will sometimes look for human food if other food is scarce, so people visiting Arctic areas where bears live should keep their food in special containers.

Near the end of hibernation, the pregnant female gives birth to two to four cubs. In spring, they come out of their den. The mother bear will take care of her cubs for at least two years. As they grow, the young ones learn the skills they will need to survive on their own. What looks like rambunctious play to us is really their way of experimenting and learning.

FACTS

About Walruses:

- Walrus males are 9 to 12 ft (2.7 to 3.6 m) long; females are 7 to 10 ft (2 to 3 m).

- Males weigh 1,640 to 3,400 lb (800 to 1,560 kg); females 1,250 to 2300 lb (570 to 1,040 kg).

- Walruses eat shellfish by sucking the meat out of the shell.

- Walruses live both in the sea and on land or ice floes; when on land or ice, they will gather in large groups, sometimes of thousands.

Seals and Walruses

Seals are shaped like torpedos, a shape that makes them clumsy on land but graceful in the water. Their rear flippers, all but useless on land, move seals swiftly while they're swimming. Their short front flippers have tiny claws to grasp their prey. Seals, like whales, have provided food, oil, and skins to Native peoples in the Arctic for many centuries.

Walruses are very big seals. They live in icy waters all around the Arctic. With their long tusks and whiskers, they look like funny old men. Their whiskers are really sensors that help them find food in the mud at the bottom of the sea. They use their tusks to pull themselves out of the water and to make breathing holes in the ice. Males use them to fight other males during breeding season. Orcas and Polar Bears have to be very careful not to be seriously injured or killed by the dangerous tusks when preying on walruses.

Walruses find their food at the bottom of the ocean. They squirt great jets of water into the ocean floor to dislodge clams and other bivalves. They hold the shellfish tight in their mouths, then suck the meat out like a great vacuum and swallow it whole.

The walrus has very thick, wrinkled skin that acts a lot like armor to protect them from attacks by other animals. A thick layer of blubber insulates them from the frigid temperatures of Arctic waters.

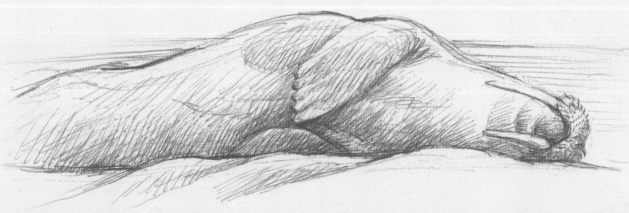

Other Arctic Animals

The Arctic tundra is home to a great variety of land mammals, many of which have white fur in winter that turns darker in summer. This allows them to blend in with their surroundings all year round. Arctic land mammals also have thick fur with a shorter, dense layer next to their skin, which helps them survive the biting winter cold. Many mammals also have special oil glands that coat their fur and help keep them warm.

The Dall Sheep lives mostly in northern Alaska and in the Yukon in Canada. I once came upon a herd of Dall Sheep in an Alaska park. Knowing that they can be very shy of people, I crept along carefully, circling around so that I could look down on them. I was feeling quite pleased with just how close I had come when one of them nonchalantly got up and came within a few feet of me. I'd had no idea they could be so tame.

Dall Sheep (left) are found only in North America, but their close relative, the Snow Sheep, lives in Arctic regions of Siberia.

The beautiful Ermine (above) is a ferocious predator, eating small animals as well as insects, birds and their eggs. It is a strong swimmer and a good climber.

The Arctic Hare (below) can bound at speeds of up to forty miles (sixty kilometers) an hour.

The Arctic Hare lives in lower-lying areas of the Arctic. It has shorter ears than most hares, and large hind feet that act as snowshoes in the deep winter snow. Its claws are strong and well adapted to digging through the snow in search of food and shelter. Watching for predators, it crouches down behind a rock or mound of snow. Its ears are tucked close to its head, only its eyes visible as it scans the vast expanses. When startled, it will stand tall on its hind legs and then, like a bouncing snowball, hop off quickly across the snow.

Ermines, or Stoats, are circumpolar. They are a rich brown in summer, but they are best known for their beautiful white winter coats. This white fur was long a favorite of fur traders and European royalty.

Survival in the Arctic

People have lived in the Arctic for thousands of years. Life is difficult, and they have had to survive the frigid winter months by making use of what they could find close at hand. Traditionally, their clothes were made from animal skins. They ate whatever animals they could find, as well as the berries and plants that grew in summer. They built homes of ice and snow or of whalebone and hides. During one of my early visits, I saw a woman washing her clothes in the cold waters of a nearby stream. Life is not easy in this harsh climate.

For animals and birds that do not migrate south, finding food in the Arctic winter can be difficult. Many animals have to forage in the ice and snow.

This Polar Bear skull rests on a vast expanse of barren-looking ground, a symbol of the harshness of polar life.

These Polar Bears are fighting over a large salmon that one of them has caught. Fish are very important to the diets of people and animals in the polar regions.

Peary Caribou dig into the snow with their strong hooves to find the grasses, herbs, and other plants they like to graze on. Grizzlies use their long, sharp claws to get at food.

Of course, survival is not just about finding food. It is often about not becoming someone else's food. The Golden Plover's black-and-gold speckled coloring (right) blends in so well with the mottled terrain of the Arctic summer that you rarely see one until you have heard it calling. I once stood over a nest containing four tiny chicks for several minutes without being able to see them, because they were so well camouflaged.

Survival in the Arctic may be a challenge, but the summers, while not hot, are incredibly beautiful. The low-angled sunlight gleams on clear lakes and rivers. It lights up the bare hills and shows off the richness and variety of the rolling tundra. The first time I visited, it made me think of a Persian carpet made not out of thread, but of mosses, lichens, dwarf birch, and willows, and of many-colored flowering plants.

Caribou

Caribou are reindeer that live in North America. Reindeer are unlike other deer in that both males and females have antlers. Wild reindeer used to be found all around the Arctic, but now most of them are domesticated. Only in North America are large numbers of wild reindeer found.

The Peary Caribou is the smallest North American reindeer. It lives on the High Arctic islands, ranging over the area in large herds as it searches for its favorite foods: moss, lichen, and green plants.

The Peary Caribou's thick fur is white in winter, and darker in summer. Its many hollow hairs allow the caribou to stay afloat while swimming. Its cloven hooves are flexible and can spread wide, like snowshoes, for easier walking over the snow. These large hooves also serve as paddles in the water and can dig through the winter snow in search of lichen.

Peary Caribou are hunted mainly by wolves. They are on Canada's endangered list because their numbers have gone down drastically over the past twenty years. Scientists aren't sure why this is so, but it may be due to an increase in wolf populations, climate change, and more competition for food from musk oxen.

The Peary Caribou's antlers are very large and covered in a soft fuzz called "velvet." The velvet is dark in color, but when stripped off, the antler beneath is pure white.

Wolf cubs are completely helpless when born, and depend on both parents for food and protection for about a year.

Arctic Wolves

Arctic Wolves live in the frigid lands of the High Arctic, where the ground often stays frozen all year. To make sure that they get enough to eat, wolf packs range over an area as wide as 800 square miles (2,000 hectares). They are fairly small compared to other wolves, and their ears are shorter, which helps protect them against the cold.

Arctic Wolves live in small packs, usually including the mother, the father, and the young (up to two or three years old). Their main food is musk oxen and caribou, but they will also eat small animals like rabbits and ground squirrels. When hunting large animals, the wolves gather together to form large packs. They single out the older and weaker members of the herd, since they will be easier to catch. By weeding out the more vulnerable animals, the wolves help keep the musk ox and caribou herds healthy and strong.

Because they live in areas too cold for people to live in, Arctic Wolves are not endangered—unlike their relatives in warmer climates, which are often hunted by humans.

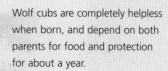

FACTS About Arctic Wolves:

- Arctic Wolves stand 2 to 3 ft (60 to 90 cm) tall and are 3 to 5 ft (1 to 1.5 m) long from their heads to the base of their tails.

- They weigh up to 175 lb (80 kg). The female is lighter than the male.

- Arctic Wolves live only in the Canadian Arctic and northern Greenland.

- Because the ground is usually frozen and cannot be dug, Arctic Wolves often use caves as dens.

- The mother gives birth to 2 or 3 pups in late spring—a small litter compared to other wolves.

- The average lifespan of the Arctic Wolf in the wild is 7 years (in captivity, they have been known to reach 17 years).

Arctic Whales

Whales are mammals that live in the ocean. Instead of fur, whales have very thick skin and a layer of fat, called blubber, that acts as insulation to keep them warm in cold water.

The Beluga Whale is called the "sea canary" because it sings with a voice that includes squeaks, whistles, clicks, chirps, and trills. Its name means "white one" in Russian, but young Belugas are gray. This makes it hard for predators, like Polar Bears and Orcas, to see them. Like other whales, Belugas travel in groups called pods. They feed on herring and cod, squid, and octopus. Their small teeth are not made for chewing, but for grabbing their prey, which they swallow whole.

I confess that I find the Narwhal a little uninteresting, except for its tusk, which is a marvel. The male's left front tooth grows up to eight feet (2.5 meters) long, making it look like a sea-going unicorn. It may look like a dangerous weapon, but the Narwhal's tusk is really a very sensitive instrument. More than ten million tiny nerves run through it. This lets the whale sense the quality of the water it is swimming in, including temperature, amount of salt, water pressure, and evidence of other creatures.

The Bowhead Whale is named for its unusual mouth, which is shaped like a bow. This largest of all Arctic whales has long been prized by hunters for its blubber, meat, oil, and bones. Once found in large numbers throughout the Arctic, it is now endangered. Hunting Bowheads is prohibited, except by Native peoples who hunt them for food.

(Above) The spiral shape of a Narwhal's tusk is like something out of a fantasy tale. The tusk was once thought to contain magical properties.

Small and white, the Beluga Whale (below) always looks like it has a smile on its face.

FACTS About Arctic Whales:

- The Narwhal averages 13 ft (4 m) in length and weighs almost 2 tons.

- Narwhals sometimes get trapped under the ice and die.

- Female Narwhals only rarely grow a tusk, and it is much shorter than the male's.

- Female Bowhead Whales give birth only every 3 to 6 years, to a single calf.

- Beluga Whales are 13 to 16 ft (4 to 5 m) long.

- Beluga Whales winter where there is open water or shifting ice, and move further north for the summer.

The Bowhead (above) is the largest of the Arctic whales, at sixty feet (eighteen meters) long and 100 tons. It lives on a diet of krill and other small sea creatures.

Puffins

Puffins are charming, stubby black-and-white birds. With their puffy cheeks, bright orange webbed feet, and large, brightly colored bills, they are hard to miss. Their short wings make flying a challenge. To take off, they throw themselves off high cliffs, dropping down to gain enough speed to fly. Underwater, though, their wings are marvelous paddles. You could say that the birds fly through water. Their oddly shaped bills have a special use, too. In them, the puffins can catch and carry as many as thirty small fish at once!

Tufted Puffins and Horned Puffins breed in the cold waters of the northern Pacific Ocean, which includes the Arctic Sea. The Tufted Puffin has a bright orange bill and very flashy feather tufts swept back over its head like elaborate eyebrows. The Horned Puffin has a bright yellow bill. Along with the fish that all puffins eat, Horned Puffins also eat small squid and crustaceans.

The Atlantic Puffin is known for its large, multi-colored bill. Atlantic Puffins breed on islands in the northern Atlantic Ocean. They move south for the winter, where they live and fish out on the ocean, far from land.

Puffins nest in underground burrows. They choose a place near the island's edge so they can easily escape gulls that try to steal their eggs. Only one egg is laid each year, and both parents care for the egg and the young chick. Since puffins breed in large colonies, you can easily find hundreds of them—often several species at once—nesting together.

Puffins use their webbed feet for swimming on the surface of the water, but their wings take over when they are under water.

FACTS About Puffins:

- The colorful outer covering of their bills is the puffins' most notable feature during breeding season. In winter, it is shed and replaced by a duller covering.

- Puffins also molt their feathers, becoming less vividly colored.

- Their diet makes the smell around a puffin breeding colony very unpleasant—imagine the stench of hundreds or thousands of birds that eat nothing but fish!

- The life expectancy of the Atlantic Puffin is close to 20 years, but since they have only one chick each year, the population can be easily threatened if many chicks perish in one season.

Other Arctic Birds

Arctic birds are amazing. Many of them live in, over, and near water. Most of them eat sea animals, including fish and crustaceans, but there are also birds of prey, like the Snowy Owl and the Gyrfalcon, that hunt small land animals. There is even the occasional songbird, like the Snow Bunting.

The Long-tailed Jaeger is an elegant-looking bird of prey. It has two long feathers that extend from its tail, as long as ten inches (twenty-five centimeters). It flies quickly, like a falcon, and hunts both fish and small land mammals. The Jaeger is also a thief, stealing food from other birds.

Murres are related to puffins and, like their relatives, they feed on many kinds of small sea life. They are famous for swimming at least one thousand miles (1,600 kilometers) of their yearly migration, which can be a total of six thousand miles (9,600 kilometers). They swim because their chicks, only three and a half weeks old at the beginning of the migration, cannot fly yet.

The Siberian Crane (right) is a tall, elegant crane that breeds across Arctic Siberia. It winters on the Yangtze River in China, and in Iran. The Siberian Crane is endangered, both because of hunting and the loss of its wetland habitat. Many people are working hard to preserve this bird through captive breeding programs and by trying to save wetlands.

Jaegers (above) are graceful in flight and can hover in mid-air. When their nests are threatened, they will glide down with their wings curved, calling out a warning to the intruder.

(Right) Kittiwakes (a type of gull), murres, and puffins (the three species appear top to bottom) are often found together in colonies. The kittiwakes will take advantage by stealing food and eggs from the other birds.

Snow Geese (below) often fly non-stop for as many as 3,000 miles (4,800 kilometers) during migration. The rest of their lives, though, they rarely fly, preferring to walk and hop along the ground.

Snow Geese are found only in North America. They are completely white, but in flight you will notice that their wing tips are black. They have orange feet and an orange bill. Both geese and swans are often seen in giant flocks flying overhead. Geese spend as much time foraging in fields as they do in water, while swans tend to prefer lakes and ponds.

Tundra Swans breed in the Arctic. Their bills are black and their all-white wings help you tell them from geese in flight. With their long necks, these swans can eat plants up to three feet (one meter) below the surface of the water. The Tundra Swan is sometimes called Whistling Swan in North America because of the sound its wings make. The beating of its wings is so loud it can be heard clearly even when the swan is 165 feet (50 meters) above the ground.

There are also many species of gulls and their relatives, skuas, throughout the Arctic. They can catch their own fish, but these opportunists often congregate in places where other birds breed, hoping to steal an egg or a young hatchling.

Tundra Swans (right) with their cygnets in the nest.

In the
ANTARCTIC

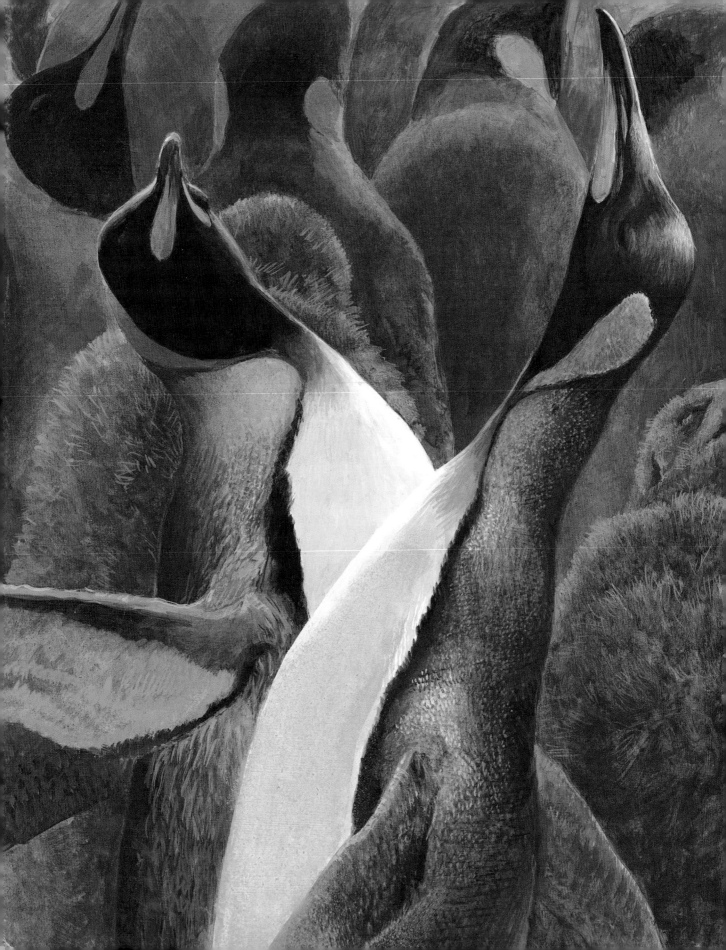

Penguins

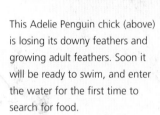

When I set out on my first visit to Antarctica, I expected to see lots of penguins, but I was astounded by how many we saw. There were thousands gathered together all along the coastal areas where our ship went, and they were joined by other birds and by seals. The shores were littered with wildlife.

Penguins are all mostly black and white, but some have orange or red feet and some have some coloring along their bills, like Emperor Penguins and Gentoo Penguins. The Macaroni Penguin has a fancy headdress of yellow feathers sweeping back from its eyes.

A thick layer of blubber and small, closely set feathers help keep penguins warm and dry. They can't fly and are a bit clumsy on land or when sliding across the ice on their stomachs, but they are graceful swimmers. Some ride the waves to shore, then jump out onto land. Adelie Penguins leap over the waves while they swim.

The Emperor Penguin is a standout, and not just because of its size. It is the only penguin that spends the winter in Antarctica.

This Adelie Penguin chick (above) is losing its downy feathers and growing adult feathers. Soon it will be ready to swim, and enter the water for the first time to search for food.

These King Penguins (opposite) are trying to attract a mate by showing off their colorful heads and necks. While displaying, they will also give a trumpet-like call.

The Royal Penguin (left) is one of several crested penguins found around the Antarctic Ocean.

These Emperor Penguins (above) are taking a break from walking the long distance to their breeding grounds by tobogganing on their stomachs.

(Opposite) Chinstrap Penguins are the most common penguins in Antartica. There are more than ten million!

The male Emperor Penguin incubates the egg deposited on his feet by the female. He covers it with a loose flap of skin and feathers to keep it warm. He stands there protecting the egg during the coldest part of winter, eating nothing for two whole months. The female journeys back to sea, as much as 75 miles (120 kilometers) away, to feed. She returns in early spring with food for the hatched chick. The male then travels to the sea, where he eats his first meal in weeks before taking more food back to the chick.

Penguins choose very different places to nest. The Chinstrap Penguin, named for the streak of black around its chin, chooses the highest regions, which are the first to warm up in the spring. The Adelie Penguin, the classic "tuxedo" penguin, breeds in rocky areas, using pebbles to build well-drained nests high above mud and muck. Young penguins' downy feathers are not waterproof, and they don't have blubber to keep them warm. The nesting site plays a big part in protecting them until they can fend for themselves.

What really amazed me when I first travelled to a penguin breeding ground was that the birds, gathered together in the thousands, were not the least bit interested in us. One day I sat on the ground sketching while lines of penguins streamed by me, totally unconcerned. I painted these Chinstrap Penguins just as you see them here, coming straight at me and then veering slightly to get by.

FACTS About Penguins:

- Hundreds of Gentoo Penguins work together to fish for food, forming "rafts" at sea to help catch prey.

- Emperor Penguins can grow up to 3 ft 4" (1 m) tall and weigh 88 lb (40 kg).

- Penguins can drink salt water because they have a special organ that filters the salt into their bloodstream. They get rid of the excess salt through their noses.

- The male Emperor Penguin loses up to one-third of his body weight while caring for his chick. If he loses too much weight before the female returns, he may abandon the chick to save his own life.

Albatrosses

Crossing the ocean by boat to Antarctica can be fairly rough, but on one trip we were lucky to have a smooth journey. This meant we didn't have to worry about staying on our feet, so we were able to enjoy watching birds that were following the ship. Among these ocean-going birds, the albatross is the most magnificent.

Albatrosses spend all of their time at sea, flying in the strong, cool wind currents blowing along the waves. They come ashore only to breed, which they do every two years. While they can stay in the air for an amazingly long time,

they don't spend all their time flying. During one of my voyages in Antarctica, my shipmates and I were delighted when a Gray-headed Albatross flew on board ship and settled there for a rest.

Albatrosses eat squid, fish, and other sea creatures, and are known to scavenge for food. They were very familiar to sailors, whose ships they would follow, hoping for scraps. Some people believe that sailors considered it bad luck to harm an albatross. This is not true. In fact, sailors often killed them for food and for sport.

The greatest tragedy now for albatrosses is industrial longline fishing. Thousands of baited lines are put into the water each day to catch fish, but more than three hundred thousand seabirds are killed by them each year. Longline fishing has only been popular for twenty years or so, but it has already brought albatrosses near to extinction.

The Wandering Albatross (above), seen here on its nest, is the largest of the albatrosses and has the biggest wingspan of any bird on Earth, nearly twelve feet (3.6 meters). It is often called "tube nose" because of its long, tube-like nostrils.

(Below) This is a sketch I made of the Gray-headed Albatross that rested on board our ship.

Survival in Antarctica

T he best way to survive Antarctica is to leave in
winter, when temperatures can go down below
−110°F (−79°C). Even in summer the temperature
barely goes above freezing. What may surprise
you is that Antarctica is a desert, getting less than two
inches (five centimeters) of precipitation each year.
Its blizzards are not made up of fresh snow, but mostly
of already fallen snow whipped around by fierce winds.
We may think that Antarctica and the Arctic are alike, but
they are very different. After all, the Arctic has the world's
largest bear, the Polar Bear, but the largest land animal
in Antarctica is a wingless mosquito.

This painting shows two penguins
sheltering among dozens of whale
bones left over from days when
Antarctic whales were hunted
nearly to extinction.

This leucistic (white) Gentoo Penguin was being attacked by two Giant Petrels hoping for a meal. They noticed that the penguin was different, and assumed it would be weak. Happily, they were disappointed. The little fellow held them off until they finally gave up and went away.

Penguins contend with many dangers in their struggle to survive. They must guard against the skua, a seabird that eats penguin eggs and chicks. Leopard Seals lie in wait just under the ice, ready to grab an unwary penguin as it enters the water. Weather can also be an enemy. If it gets cold too early in the winter, the penguins may die before they can migrate. If it warms up too soon, the ice may melt before young chicks are ready to swim.

If you go to Antarctica, chances are you won't see any krill, even though they are the most important living creatures there. These tiny, shrimp-like crustaceans are about two inches (five centimeters) long. They swarm in the ocean by the thousands, and are the main food of penguins, fish, seals, and whales. Without krill, none of these animals would survive.

Krill

The Snow Petrel is a small seabird that eats krill, as well as fish and other small shellfish. It is unusual because it can survive in the Antarctic all year. It breeds on the mainland and moves to ice floes in winter. It is so well adapted to the Antarctic cold that it would die in warmer temperatures. When threatened by predators, the Snow Petrel ejects a stream of foul-smelling, oily, half-digested krill—a very effective way to get rid of unwelcome guests!

39

Seals in Antarctica

Southern Elephant Seals are the largest seals in the world. They dive very deep for their food, 3,200 feet (1,000 meters) or more, and can stay underwater for as long as two hours. They breed in huge colonies, but each male claims his own territory within the colony by roaring and fighting. The females then come ashore to give birth. There can be more than one thousand seals in a breeding colony, and the most prominent males might have fifty mates.

Male Elephant Seals have a large proboscis that looks like a huge, blobby nose. It helps them make a noise like a very, very loud raspberry, to warn off other males during mating season.

Leopard Seals are more solitary than Elephant Seals. They are smaller, too, and eat in shallower waters. The favorite food of adults is penguins, while smaller seals eat krill, squid, and fish. Leopard Seals catch penguins by staying quietly just under the surface of the water. When the penguin enters the water, the seal grabs it and shakes it vigorously by the feet until it comes right out of its skin! It then eats the penguin while the skin drifts away.

(Below) Fur Seals were once hunted for their fur, and they became very rare. There are more now, but the seal population has not fully recovered. Here, a Fur Seal rests next to an old whaling boat. Just out of sight, old whalebones are scattered along the beach.

FACTS About Seals:

- Adult male Elephant Seals can be as big as 20 ft (6 m) and weigh nearly 6,000 lb (2,700 kg); females are much smaller, up to 10 ft (3 m) and 2,000 lb (900 kg).

- Leopard Seal males are around 9 ft (2.8 m) long and weigh about 700 lb (320 kg); females are nearly 10 ft (3 m) long and 800 lb (360 kg).

- Leopard Seals are very aggressive, and have even been known to threaten people.

- There are six species of seal in Antarctica.

(Right) A swimming
Leopard Seal.

These young Elephant Seals (above)
have not yet developed the huge
proboscises they will have as adults.

Whales in Antarctica

In some ways, the story of humans in Antarctica is really the story of whales. For many decades, whales were hunted for food and oil, and many species were nearly destroyed. Fortunately, the danger was recognized, and now the waters surrounding Antarctica have been declared a whale sanctuary. Whale fishing is closely monitored.

There are two types of whales: toothed whales and baleen whales. Toothed whales eat fish, squid, and small sea mammals. Baleen whales have a "baleen" instead of teeth. The baleen looks like a comb and helps the whale to eat enormous amounts of food. It opens its mouth and takes in lots of fish and crustaceans. When it closes its mouth, the water is filtered out through the baleen, then the whale swallows the food.

Orcas, or Killer Whales, are one of only two species of toothed whales in Antarctica. They are beautiful, with their contrasting black and white coloring. Graceful and athletic, they can leap straight up into the air, landing in the water with a mighty splash. They often cooperate to capture prey—one member of the pod will tip an ice floe up, dislodging a resting seal, while others wait below for the unsuspecting victim.

Humpback Whales are baleen whales. These medium-sized whales can take in around five thousand pounds (2,270 kilograms) of krill every day. In this picture (right), the two Humpback Whales look tiny compared with the huge mountain of ice behind them.

Orcas travel in pods of close family members. All members of the pod help care for the young.

FACTS About Antarctic Whales:

- Whales are the only mammals adapted to life in the open sea.

- All species of Antarctic whales can be found in oceans throughout the world.

- Orcas are often called Killer Whales. It is true that they are members of the whale family, like porpoises and dolphins, but their closest relation is the dolphin.

- The Right Whale, a baleen whale found in Antarctica, is rich in blubber, and fairly easy to catch. It also doesn't sink when killed, so at one time it was considered the "right" whale to hunt.

Migration at the Poles

Most of the animals and birds living near the poles migrate to escape the extreme winter cold. Their migrating habits, though, are not all the same. Extreme weather can lead to some extreme migrations. Some travel very short distances, but others take amazing journeys.

The Arctic Tern must be addicted to sunlight. It breeds in the long days of the Arctic summer, then flies all the way to the edges of Antarctica for the south polar summer—a total distance of more than twenty thousand miles (32,000 kilometers) each year! This is the longest migration of any animal in the world. The Tern's young fly south with their parents and stay alone in Antarctica for two years. Then they are ready to begin the annual migration. Like their parents, they spend the rest of their lives seeking the sun.

Arctic Terns (below) build their nests on open rocks close to the sea. They protect the nest fiercely, and may dive-bomb people in boats too close to shore.

Wilson's Storm Petrel takes the opposite course from the Arctic Tern, and travels a shorter distance. It breeds in the Antarctic in summer and winters in and over the waters of the northern Atlantic Ocean. Other birds, like penguins, migrate to lands much closer to their breeding grounds.

When skimming or hovering over the sea looking for food, Wilson's Storm Petrel (above) patters with its feet as if running along the surface of the water.

Most whales summer in the colder regions to take advantage of the great abundance of food. Humpback Whales summer in both Arctic and Antarctic waters, eating huge amounts of krill, fish, and other sea creatures. They move to warm tropical waters to breed, surviving only on their reserves of fat until they return to their feeding grounds. The northern and southern Humpbacks never meet, each group remaining on its own side of the equator.

Many Arctic land mammals migrate, too. Caribou follow a traditional migration pattern, moving south during the winter and returning north to breed. The Polar Bear travels wherever there are Ringed Seals. In times when food is scarce, the bears may enter northern towns, where they scavenge garbage left by humans.

Some Arctic birds and animals do not migrate at all, or move only very short distances. The Willow Ptarmigan is a lovely bird that lives its entire life on the tundra. It marks the seasons by changing its plumage from dark in summer to white in winter. It sometimes moves slightly southward in the coldest months, but does not really migrate. It survives the winter by eating twigs and buds—it is especially partial to willows.

Epilogue

I have watched animals all my life, both in far-off places like Antarctica and in my own backyard. What always intrigues me is how the animals survive in their habitat. The extreme temperatures of the two polar regions present unique challenges to their inhabitants. The winters are brutal, food can be scarce, and their young are especially vulnerable. Nearly all polar creatures must also contend with their natural enemies, fierce predators that are often preyed upon by even larger predators. Climate change is also a threat to the animals at the poles.

Animals in the Arctic and Antarctica have been over-hunted by humans. Some are killed by industrial fishing. Global warming is changing the balance of the climate. Ice caps are shrinking, threatening the animals that depend on that ice as part of their life cycle. In the past, the whales of Antarctica were saved from extinction by human effort. Now, some longline fisheries color their bait blue to prevent albatrosses and other sea animals from eating it. Otherwise, they might get caught in the nets and drown. Other solutions can be found if we continue to work at it. We just need to try.

My journeys to the Arctic and Antarctica have taught me that beauty can be found in the most unexpected places. The Arctic, a world of white in winter, is washed with color in the summer: lichens, flowers, low flowering shrubs, and wildlife, like the Harlequin Duck with its rich plumage, brighten the landscape. Nowhere else on Earth can you stand in one spot and see almost a million living creatures, and yet in Antarctica during breeding season there are penguins as far as the eye can see. These areas are fantastical scenes. We should celebrate their beauty and the great variety of life that not only survives, but thrives in the Arctic and Antarctica.

   People often say that variety is the spice of life. By this they mean that life would be boring if everything were the same. But I think that variety is more than the spice of life. It is life itself. Without all the different kinds of creatures and plants, the world would no longer be alive. It is up to us to preserve beauty and variety everywhere in the world. Perhaps this is most important in our two Polar Worlds.

—Robert Bateman

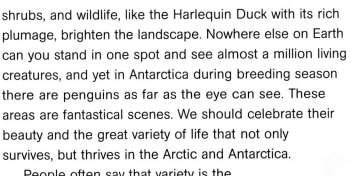

(Below) King Penguin chicks

Glossary

Arctic Circle—An imaginary line around the globe, 66 degrees north of the equator.

Bivalve—Shellfish with a hinged two-part shell, like clams, mussels, and oysters.

Blubber—A thick layer of fat under the skin of mammals like whales, penguins, and seals.

Circumpolar—Refers to the area surrounding the North and South Poles (see Polar regions).

Crustaceans—Mostly sea-dwelling animals, like lobsters, crabs, shrimp and krill, with protective shells on the outside instead of skeletons.

Glacier—A large sheet or river of ice, made from compacted snow, that moves slowly over the landscape.

Iceberg—A large floating chunk of ice broken away from a glacier.

Ice Caps—Large, dome-shaped ice normally formed over land. Polar ice caps are found over the two Poles (so the Arctic Polar Ice Cap is formed over water, not land).

Ice floe—A chunk of floating sea ice.

Lichen—Composite organisms made up of fungi combined with algae. Able to survive extreme cold, they grow on rocks and trees.

Polar regions—The extremely cold areas surrounding the North and South Poles. They have less sunlight than anywhere else on Earth.

Proboscis—A long, flexible snout, like the trunk of an elephant or the snout of the Elephant Seal.

Sea Ice—Ice formed from ocean water, unlike glaciers and icebergs, which are made of compacted snow.

Tree line—The line beyond which the climate is too cold and the growing season too short for trees to grow.

Tundra—Land beyond the tree line, where only small plants and shrubs grow. The Arctic tundra extends around the globe. The Antarctic tundra is more limited and has fewer plants and no native mammals.

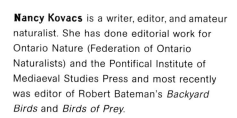

Nancy Kovacs is a writer, editor, and amateur naturalist. She has done editorial work for Ontario Nature (Federation of Ontario Naturalists) and the Pontifical Institute of Mediaeval Studies Press and most recently was editor of Robert Bateman's *Backyard Birds* and *Birds of Prey*.

Polar Worlds was produced by Madison Press Books

Art Director: Diana Sullada

Production Manager: Sandra L. Hall
Vice President, Finance and Production: Susan Barrable

Associate Publisher: Alison Maclean
President and Publisher: Oliver Salzmann